文憑養不出領袖

治理是一門藝術

Diplomas Don't Create Leaders; Governance Is an Art

Ping Xu 徐萍

前言Preface

這本書挑戰一個社會幻覺：高分與文憑能帶來真正的領導力。
我用「分數怪物」來形容一個病態制度，它把人訓練成
考試機器，卻無法培養出能應對現實的公民。
我也用「文憑蠢貨」來命名一種現象：那些靠著耀眼學歷進入
權力核心的人，缺乏治理的智慧，卻沉迷於數字與修辭。
這並不是情緒化的辱罵，而是對文明退化的提醒。
當教育被簡化為分數，領導被簡化為文憑，人類並非在進步，
而是在倒退。真正的領導，不是演算數據的能力，
而是面對現實、整合人心與開創未來的勇氣。

This book challenges a dangerous illusion: that high scores and diplomas guarantee true leadership.
I use the term “Score Monsters” to describe a pathological system that trains children into exam machines but fails to produce citizens capable of facing reality. I also use “Diploma Fools” to name a phenomenon: people who rise to power through prestigious credentials yet lack the wisdom to govern, lost in numbers and rhetoric.
These terms are not insults but reminders of civilizational regression. When education is reduced to scores and leadership to diplomas, humanity is not advancing but retreating. True leadership is not about data or prestige, but about the courage to face reality, integrate society, and create new futures.

第一章
分數與文憑的陷阱

Chapter 1:
The Trap of Scores and Diplomas

第一節 分數怪物
Section 1: The Score Monsters

教育的本意應該是培養完整的人，然而在許多國家，
教育早已淪為「分數生產線」。孩子的價值被等同於
考卷上的數字，學習的目標被簡化為「考高分」。
在這樣的體制裡，好奇心被扼殺，思考被縮減成解題公式，
合作被犧牲在競爭之下。父母焦慮、老師無奈、
學生窒息，全社會陷入分數的魔咒。
所謂「分數怪物」，不是孩子本身，而是這個制度的畸形產物。
它塑造出的是「高分機器」，而非真正能面對現實挑戰的人。
這些人或許能進名校，卻缺乏想像力與創造力。
文明因此沒有向前，而是走向退化。

Education is meant to nurture whole human beings, yet in many countries it has devolved into a “score factory.” A child’s worth is equated with exam numbers, and the goal of learning reduced to “getting higher scores.”
In such a system, curiosity is strangled, thinking shrinks into formulas, and cooperation is sacrificed for competition. Parents grow anxious, teachers are powerless, students suffocate—the entire society falls under the spell of scores.
“Score Monsters” are not the children themselves but the system’s grotesque creations. What emerges are “high-score machines,” not individuals equipped for real-life challenges. They may enter elite universities, but they lack imagination and creativity. Civilization thus moves not forward, but backward.

第二節 文憑蠢貨
Section 2: The Diploma Fools

當「分數怪物」成長進入社會，他們往往依靠
學歷的光環進入權力核心。
於是我們看到另一種現象：「文憑蠢貨」。
這些人憑藉名校文憑取得權威，卻把治理當成考試，
把政策當成標準答案。他們熟悉數據、會背理論，
卻無法傾聽、無法整合、更無法創造。
結果不是解決問題，
而是讓問題更加僵化。
更嚴重的是，文憑蠢貨本身掉入了「工作＝收入」
的盲腸制度。他們深信社會運作就該像考試一樣，
以「努力換取成績，以勞動換取收入」。因此：
他們只能 複製制度，而不是創造新制度；
他們無法理解 無條件分配 的政策
（如 UBI、全民健保、長照公共化）；
他們把改革簡化為 績效考核（KPI、指標、排名），
追求漂亮的「成績單」而非真正的改變；
他們陷入 數據幻象，把人民的痛苦排除在統計之外。
這樣的治理邏輯，本質上是「分數社會」的延伸。
文憑蠢貨無法引導改革，因為他們正是盲腸制度的
守門人與複製品。

When “Score Monsters” grow up and enter society, they often ride the aura of their diplomas into positions of power. This gives rise to another phenomenon: the “Diploma Fools.”

These individuals wield elite degrees as authority but treat governance like an exam and policies like standardized answers. They know data, they recite theories, but they cannot listen, integrate, or create. The result is not problem-solving but deeper paralysis.

Worse still, diploma fools are trapped in the blind system of “work = income.” They believe society must function like an exam: “effort equals score, labor equals income.” As a result:

They replicate systems rather than create new ones.

They cannot imagine unconditional policies such as UBI, universal healthcare, or public long-term care.

They reduce reform to performance assessments (KPIs, indicators, rankings), seeking a glossy “report card” instead of real change.

They fall into the illusion of data, excluding human suffering from their statistics.

This logic of governance is merely an extension of the score-driven society. Diploma fools cannot lead reform because they are the guardians and replicas of the very system that needs dismantling.

第二章
高學歷治國的失敗

Chapter 2:
The Failure of
Credentialed Governance

2016 年脫歐公投之後，英國迎來數年動盪。食品短缺、
港口塞車、貨架空空，原本承諾的「獨立自主」
淪為物流與貿易的混亂。推動脫歐的，
多是牛劍菁英政客，他們能言善道，
但在現實操作中卻顯得無能。
這場混亂揭示了高學歷政客在治理上的真實面貌：
會做辯論，不會做治理。

After the 2016 Brexit referendum, Britain entered years of turmoil. Food shortages, port gridlocks, and empty supermarket shelves replaced promises of “sovereignty.” The architects of Brexit were largely Oxbridge elites—eloquent debaters but inept managers. The chaos exposed the reality of credentialed governance: skilled in rhetoric, incapable in practice.

社會往往相信「高學歷＝治理力」。但當這些文憑菁英
真正執政時，卻一再證明：他們能拿高分，
卻無法解決高風險。從英國到美國、印度，
案例清楚顯示：學歷光環掩蓋了治理上的軟弱與無能。

Societies often assume “higher education = higher capacity to govern.” Yet when diploma elites take power, they repeatedly prove otherwise: they can ace exams but cannot manage crises. From Britain to the U.S. to India, case studies reveal how the glow of credentials masks weakness in governance.

案例分析 Real Cases

案例一：英國——脫歐的治理災難

脫歐派的牛劍政客，把複雜的國際經貿談判簡化成「要或不要」的口號。結果現實報復很快到來：企業搬離英國，倫敦金融中心地位受損，漁民出口受阻。這些政客善於辯論，卻完全低估治理的細節成本。

Oxbridge politicians driving Brexit reduced complex international negotiations into a yes-or-no slogan. Reality soon struck back: companies relocated, London’s financial hub weakened, fishermen struggled with blocked exports. These leaders excelled at debating but underestimated the true costs of governance.

案例二：美國——常春藤的醫療與住房困局

美國的醫療支出佔 GDP 比例世界第一，
但常春藤背景的決策者卻無法阻止
病人因醫療破產。房價與租金持續上升，
無家可歸者遍布大城市。
政客的解方依然是厚厚的報告與空泛的聽證會，
而不是具體可行的改革。

The U.S. spends more on healthcare as a share of GDP than any other nation, yet Ivy-trained policymakers cannot prevent medical bankruptcies. Housing costs soar, homelessness spreads across major cities. Their solutions remain thick reports and endless hearings, not concrete reforms.

案例三：印度——學術總理的沉默與無力

曼莫漢．辛格，牛津與劍橋學歷，享有「世界級經濟學者」的名聲。但在他十年總理任內，腐敗醜聞層出不窮，他卻選擇沉默。人民譏諷他是「沒有聲音的領導者」，證明了學術光環無法掩蓋治理的軟弱。

Manmohan Singh, with Oxford and Cambridge credentials and global stature as an economist, served a decade as India's prime minister. Yet corruption scandals multiplied under his watch, and he remained silent. Derided as the "silent leader," Singh's tenure proved that academic brilliance cannot hide governance weakness.

英國的牛劍政客，把國家當成辯論賽；
美國的常春藤政客，把危機當成政策模擬；
印度的學術總理，則把沉默當成治理。
三種表現不同，但共同點一致：
高學歷無法轉化成高效能治理。

Britain's Oxbridge politicians treated the nation like a debating stage; America's Ivy elites treated crises like policy simulations; India's academic prime minister treated silence as governance. Different styles, but one shared truth: higher education does not translate into higher governance performance.

啟示 Conclusion

高學歷治國的失敗，提醒我們不要再把國家當作「文憑菁英的試驗場」。
人民需要的不是履歷最漂亮的政客，
而是懂得面對現實、
敢於承擔責任的領導者。

The failure of credentialed governance warns us not to treat nations as playgrounds for diploma elites. Citizens do not need the prettiest résumés in politics—they need leaders who face reality and shoulder responsibility.

第三章
分數邏輯的政治後果

Chapter 3:
The Political Consequences of Score Logic

在台灣的立法院，一場有關少子化的聽證會正在進行。
官員們展示精美的投影片，列出「補助金額」、「政策方案」、
「績效指標」，數字整齊得像考卷答案。然而，
現場一名年輕媽媽卻站起來質問：「請問你們哪一位官員，
有真正排過托嬰中心的候補名單？」全場沉默。
這正是分數邏輯的後果：制度滿口數字，卻無法觸及生活。

At Taiwan's Legislative Yuan, a hearing on declining fertility was underway. Officials presented polished slides filled with "subsidy amounts," "policy schemes," and "performance indicators"—as neat as exam answers. Then a young mother stood up and asked: "Has any of you ever actually waited on a childcare center's waiting list?" The room fell silent. This is the outcome of score logic: systems fluent in numbers but deaf to life.

「分數邏輯」是一種深植於教育制度的思維：
凡事都有標準答案，只要背對了題庫，就能拿高分。
當這種思維滲入政治，後果是：
政策被簡化成「數字競賽」；
治理變成「績效表演」；
人民的真實需求被忽視。

"Score logic" is a mindset ingrained by exam-driven education: every problem has a standard answer, and memorizing the right template earns high marks. When this mindset seeps into politics, the results are:
Policies reduced to a "numbers contest."
Governance turned into a "performance show."
Citizens' real needs left ignored.

案例分析 Real Cases

案例一：日本——少子化對策的數字遊戲

日本政府連年推出少子化對策，每次都附上「增加多少補助」、「設立多少托育名額」的數字。可結果是什麼？出生率持續下滑。因為真正的問題是工時過長、養育成本高昂，這些卻沒有被觸動。

The Japanese government repeatedly announced anti-declining birthrate measures, each with figures for "more subsidies" or "new childcare slots." The result? Fertility rates kept falling. The real problems—excessive work hours and high child-rearing costs—remained untouched.

案例二：韓國——補助不斷，危機更深

韓國的生育補助金世界少見地高，但年輕人依然選擇不婚不育。因為他們不缺一次性的獎勵，而是需要住房保障與勞動尊嚴。政客卻沉迷於用「金額數字」來證明政績，完全無法逆轉趨勢。

Korea offers some of the world's most generous childbirth subsidies, yet young people still opt out of marriage and parenthood. They don't need one-time rewards; they need secure housing and dignity at work. Politicians, obsessed with "budget numbers" as proof of achievement, fail to reverse the trend.

案例三：美國——醫療改革的績效表演

美國醫改辯論中，政客最愛秀的是
「節省多少成本」、「多少人納入健保」。
但現實卻是醫療費用持續飆升，
數百萬人依舊因病破產。數字漂亮，人民卻破產。

In U.S. healthcare debates, politicians highlight "costs saved" or "millions newly covered." Yet costs keep soaring and millions still face medical bankruptcy. The numbers look impressive, but citizens go bankrupt.

分數邏輯的政治，就是把國家當作「大考場」。
官員追求的是「答案正確」
而不是「問題解決」。
結果是：
表面上：政策滿是 KPI、數字、排名。
實際上：問題依然存在，人民不斷失望。

Politics under score logic treats nations like exam halls. Officials pursue "correct answers" instead of real solutions. The outcome is:
On the surface: policies overflow with KPIs, statistics, rankings.
In reality: problems persist, citizens grow disillusioned.

啟示 Conclusion

分數邏輯是一種治理毒藥。它製造了「漂亮的數據」
卻掩蓋了「真實的痛苦」。一個真正的領導者，
必須超越分數邏輯，把政策視為生活的回應，
而不是考卷的答案。

Score logic is a poison in governance. It creates "beautiful numbers" while masking "real suffering." True leaders must transcend exam thinking, treating policies as responses to life—not answers to a test.

第四章
英國的牛劍困局

Chapter 4:
Britain's Oxbridge Trap

2016 年的脫歐公投，成為英國近代史上最戲劇化的政治事件。舞台上的主角幾乎清一色是牛津、劍橋畢業的政客：鮮明口才、華麗辯論、無懈可擊的履歷。他們把「離開歐盟」描繪成簡單的選擇題，好像只要投票「Yes or No」，問題就能解決。然而，當結果塵埃落定，英國卻陷入數年的混亂與分裂。

The 2016 Brexit referendum was one of the most dramatic episodes in modern British history. The leading actors were almost all Oxford and Cambridge graduates: eloquent, polished in debate, and boasting impeccable résumés. They framed “leaving the EU” as a simple multiple-choice question, as if a Yes or No vote could settle it. But once the result came in, Britain plunged into years of turmoil and division.

牛津與劍橋培養出的是世界頂尖的辯論手、法律專家、金融人才，但這些人卻無法應付「治理」的複雜性。
脫歐證明了：菁英教育造就的不是治理者，而是修辭家。

Oxford and Cambridge have produced some of the world’s best debaters, lawyers, and financiers. Yet these elites proved incapable of handling the complexities of governance. Brexit revealed that elite education produces rhetoricians, not governors.

案例分析 Real Cases

案例一：誤導性的脫歐承諾

領銜脫歐的牛津政客鮑里斯．強森，
揮舞著「每週 3.5 億英鎊回歸國民醫療」的口號。
但這承諾很快被證明是虛假與誤導。
群眾因為口號而投票，卻換來了醫療系統
更大的壓力。

Oxford alumnus Boris Johnson led Brexit with the slogan that leaving the EU would return "£350 million a week to the NHS." The promise was soon exposed as misleading. Citizens voted on a catchy line, only to face even greater pressure on the healthcare system.

案例二：談判無能與混亂

脫歐後，牛劍背景的首相梅伊與強森，接連在與歐盟的談判中陷入僵局。他們善於發表演說，卻無法處理關稅、邊境與貿易的複雜細節，導致協議一拖再拖，國內政治也陷入癱瘓。

After Brexit, Oxford- and Cambridge-educated leaders like Theresa May and Boris Johnson floundered in negotiations with the EU. Gifted in speeches, they failed in the gritty details of tariffs, borders, and trade, leading to endless delays and domestic paralysis.

案例三：社會分裂與制度受損

脫歐不僅是經濟問題，更撕裂了社會。年輕與老年、
倫敦與鄉村、蘇格蘭與英格蘭之間的矛盾加劇。
這些牛劍政客沒有能力整合社會，
只能繼續用修辭挑動對立。
結果是民主制度的信任進一步流失。

Brexit was not just economic—it tore society apart. Generational divides, urban-rural splits, and tensions between Scotland and England deepened. Oxbridge politicians proved unable to integrate society, resorting instead to rhetoric that fueled division. Trust in democratic institutions eroded further.

脫歐展示了一個殘酷現實：牛津、劍橋訓練的是「如何贏得辯論」，而不是「如何治理國家」。這些政客把複雜問題簡化成標語，最後卻讓國家為他們的修辭買單。

Brexit laid bare a brutal reality: Oxford and Cambridge train people "to win debates," not "to govern nations." These politicians simplified complexity into slogans, leaving the country to pay for their rhetoric.

牛劍困局提醒我們：名校文憑不僅不能保證良好治理，
還可能製造災難。因為當政治被修辭支配，
真實世界的代價將由全民承擔。

The Oxbridge trap shows us: elite diplomas not only fail to guarantee good governance, they can create disaster. When politics is ruled by rhetoric, it is ordinary people who pay the price.

第五章
美國的常春藤幻象

Chapter 5:
America’s Ivy Illusion

在華盛頓國會山莊的聽證會上，一位哈佛出身的參議員
正滔滔不絕地引用數據與模型，解釋醫療改革的成本效益。
旁邊的助理遞上最新的統計表格，他熟練地翻閱，
顯得專業無比。然而，台下的普通民眾卻
忍不住低聲抱怨：
「我們只是想要能看得起醫生，不是聽你背課本。」
這就是常春藤幻象：專業滿分，解決零分。

At a Capitol Hill hearing, a Harvard-educated senator eloquently cited data and models to explain the cost-benefit of healthcare reform. An aide handed him updated statistics, which he reviewed with polished ease. To the public, he looked impeccably professional. Yet in the gallery, citizens whispered: "We just want to see a doctor without going broke—not hear a textbook recitation." This is the Ivy League illusion: flawless expertise, zero solutions.

常春藤聯盟長期被視為美國政治的「人才庫」。
總統、參議員、大法官，履歷上幾乎
都有哈佛、耶魯、普林斯頓的名字。
這種光環讓人民以為「學術菁英必然能治理國家」。
然而現實卻是：常春藤政客擅長話術與報告，
卻無法處理現實的複雜問題。

The Ivy League has long been seen as America's political "talent pool." Presidents, senators, and Supreme Court justices often carry Harvard, Yale, or Princeton on their résumés. This pedigree creates the illusion that "academic elites must govern well." Yet the reality is stark: Ivy politicians excel at rhetoric and reports, but fail in grappling with complex realities.

案例分析 Real Cases

案例一：醫療改革的空轉

美國醫療體系支出佔 GDP 的近兩成，
居世界之冠。常春藤政客在醫改辯論中，
滿口「成本效益」與「效率提升」。
但結果是數百萬人依然因病破產，
醫療費用持續飆升。人民需要的是
可負擔的醫療，不是空洞的指標。

America's healthcare system consumes nearly one-fifth of GDP, the highest in the world. Ivy politicians dominate debates with talk of "cost efficiency" and "improving metrics." Yet millions still face medical bankruptcy, and costs keep rising. Citizens need affordable care, not abstract indicators.

案例二：住房危機的失能

哈佛與耶魯背景的政策菁英們，提出無數
「住房政策白皮書」。然而在舊金山、紐約、洛杉磯，
房價與租金依舊高不可攀，
無家可歸者人數不斷攀升。
數據再漂亮，也擋不住帳篷城市一座座冒出。

Harvard- and Yale-trained policy elites have produced countless "housing white papers." Yet in cities like San Francisco, New York, and Los Angeles, housing remains unaffordable, and homelessness rises. Beautiful numbers cannot hide the mushrooming tent cities.

案例三：社會分裂的惡化

常春藤政客在公共場合，愛用「理性討論」
與「程序正義」來回應爭議。
但當社會出現撕裂，他們卻無力修補。
2020 年總統大選後，國會暴動爆發，
正是長年制度失能與菁英斷層的反撲。

Ivy politicians pride themselves on "rational debate" and "procedural fairness." Yet when society fractures, they fail to heal divisions. The January 6 Capitol riot in 2021 was not an isolated incident but the backlash to years of systemic failure and elite detachment.

常春藤的幻象在於：他們能「說服自己」
卻無法「說服人民」。
他們的政策報告細緻完整，卻和民生需求脫節；
他們的履歷耀眼，卻無法贏得人民的信任；
他們的話術高超，卻無力阻止社會崩裂。

The Ivy League illusion lies in this: they can "convince themselves" but not "convince the people."
Their policy reports are detailed yet detached from daily life.Their résumés shine but fail to inspire trust.
Their rhetoric is polished but powerless against social collapse.

啟示
Conclusion

美國的常春藤幻象提醒我們：學術菁英未必能治理國家。當政治只剩話術與報告，國家就會失去方向。人民需要的，不是滿口專業術語的政客，而是能理解痛苦、解決問題的領導者。

The Ivy League illusion teaches us: academic elites do not necessarily govern well. When politics is reduced to rhetoric and reports, nations lose direction. What citizens need is not technocratic jargon but leaders who understand suffering and solve problems.

第六章
印度的學術總理

Chapter 6:
India’s Academic Prime Minister

在國際場合，曼莫漢．辛格總是以學者的姿態出現。
他溫文儒雅，語速緩慢，談吐嚴謹，
被譽為「世界級經濟學者」。他畢業於牛津、劍橋，
並在 IMF 擔任要職，學術與專業光環耀眼。
然而，當他成為印度總理時，人們卻逐漸發現：
這位「學術菁英」缺乏的是最基本的政治魄力。

On the world stage, Manmohan Singh often appeared as the quintessential scholar—soft-spoken, precise, and dignified. Hailed as a "world-class economist," he held degrees from Oxford and Cambridge and served in senior roles at the IMF. His academic and professional pedigree was impeccable. Yet as India's prime minister, citizens gradually discovered that this "academic elite" lacked the most essential quality of governance: political authority.

曼莫漢．辛格象徵著一種典型：高學歷光環能
帶來尊敬，卻無法保證有效治理。
他雖然是改革印度經濟的推手，
但在面對政治現實時，卻選擇沉默與退縮。
結果，他的總理任期被定義為「穩定卻無力」。

Manmohan Singh symbolizes a broader truth: academic prestige earns respect but does not guarantee effective governance. Though he was credited with liberalizing India's economy, as prime minister he defaulted to silence and passivity when confronted with political realities. His tenure became defined as "stable yet powerless."

案例分析 Real Cases

案例一：經濟改革的背影

1990 年代，辛格擔任財政部長時推動市場自由化，
打開印度與世界的貿易往來，
被視為「印度經濟奇蹟的設計師」。
但這份成就，也成為他日後被
推上總理寶座的主要理由。

In the 1990s, as finance minister, Singh spearheaded market liberalization, opening India to global trade and earning credit as the "architect of India's economic miracle." This reputation later propelled him to the prime ministership.

案例二：沉默的總理

然而在十年總理任期內，當黨內腐敗醜聞爆發、
官僚體系效率低落時，辛格選擇沉默。
他既不清理門戶，也不公開譴責，
人民譏諷他是「沒有聲音的領導者」。

Yet during his decade as prime minister, when corruption scandals engulfed his party and bureaucracy stagnated, Singh remained silent. He neither cleaned house nor voiced condemnation, earning the nickname "the silent leader."

案例三：軟弱的國家治理

辛格的專業背景讓他善於數字與經濟政策，
但在國安、外交、社會衝突上，
他缺乏決斷力。這種「學術型領導」
導致國家在關鍵時刻失去方向。

Singh's expertise made him adept in numbers and economic policy, but in matters of national security, foreign policy, and social conflict, he lacked decisiveness. This "academic style of leadership" left India directionless in critical moments.

與梅克爾相比，
辛格同樣是高學歷背景，但梅克爾能將科學訓練轉化
為務實治理；辛格則困於學術心態，選擇退縮。
這正凸顯：學歷相同，差別在於是否
能成為「生命的藝術家」。

Compared with Angela Merkel, Singh shared an elite academic background. But while Merkel translated her scientific training into pragmatic governance, Singh retreated into academic caution. This contrast underscores: with similar credentials, the difference lies in becoming an "artist of life" or remaining a diploma fool.

啟示
Conclusion

曼莫漢．辛格的案例提醒我們：治理不是寫論文，
而是承擔責任。學術菁英若沒有政治魄力，
只會成為歷史的過客。真正的領導者，
必須能超越分數與文憑，
面對現實、敢於決斷。

Singh's case reminds us: governance is not about writing papers but about shouldering responsibility. Academic elites without political courage become footnotes in history. True leadership requires transcending diplomas and scores to face reality and make decisions.

第七章
東亞的少子化死局

Chapter 7:
East Asia's Demographic Dead End

在東京的一個育兒論壇上，一名年輕母親說：
「政府每年都宣布新的補助，
但我最大的困難是下班太晚，
根本沒時間接孩子。」會場一片沉默。
因為這句話，道出了日本、韓國、台灣共同的真相：
政客們滿口補助與獎金，卻不敢觸動長工時、
低薪與高房價這些結構性問題。
結果，少子化像是死亡倒數，無情地侵蝕整個東亞。

At a parenting forum in Tokyo, a young mother remarked: “The government announces new subsidies every year, but my biggest problem is getting off work too late to pick up my child.” The room fell silent. Her words captured the shared reality of Japan, Korea, and Taiwan: politicians tout subsidies and bonuses but avoid confronting long hours, low wages, and soaring housing costs. As a result, declining fertility has become a death countdown, relentlessly eroding East Asia.

東亞的少子化危機並非突如其來，
而是政客長期無力、無膽面對結構性問題的結果。
這些高學歷政客擅長做「數字政策」：補助金額、KPI、
托育名額。但當少子化變成人口崩潰時，
數字早已無法挽救現實。

East Asia’s demographic crisis did not appear overnight. It is the outcome of credentialed politicians’ long-standing inability and unwillingness to tackle structural issues. These highly educated leaders excel at “numerical policies”: subsidies, KPIs, childcare slots. Yet once fertility collapse sets in, numbers cannot save reality.

案例分析 Real Cases

案例一：日本——補助無法阻止崩潰

日本從 1990 年代起就投入鉅額少子化對策，包含生育獎金與托兒補助。然而出生率從 1.57（1989 年）一路下滑至 1.2 以下。問題不在於補助不足，而在於長工時文化與女性被迫退出職場。

Since the 1990s, Japan has poured massive funds into fertility measures, including childbirth bonuses and childcare subsidies. Yet the birthrate fell from 1.57 (1989) to below 1.2. The real issue is not insufficient subsidies but entrenched overwork culture and women being forced out of the workforce.

案例二：韓國——世界最貴的生育補助

韓國的育兒補助金額位居全球前列，
政府甚至推動
「百萬韓元育兒支票」。
但出生率在 2023 年降到 0.72，
創世界最低。原因在於房價高漲、職場壓榨，
讓年輕人乾脆選擇不婚不育。

Korea offers some of the world's most generous childcare subsidies, even distributing "million-won baby checks." Yet in 2023, its fertility rate dropped to 0.72—the lowest in the world. The cause lies in soaring housing costs and exploitative workplaces, prompting young people to forgo marriage and parenthood altogether.

案例三：台灣——政策口號的空轉

台灣政府提出「生一胎補助一胎」，
再加上月領育兒津貼，卻無法阻止出生率跌破 1。
年輕人面對低薪與高房價時，
只能說：「補助根本買不起一間房。」
少子化已經成為國安危機，
但政客依舊沉迷於短期政策。

Taiwan introduced "cash for each child" schemes and monthly childcare allowances, yet the birthrate still dropped below 1. Young people facing low wages and high housing prices say, "The subsidy doesn't even buy half a room." Fertility decline has become a national security crisis, but politicians remain obsessed with short-term measures.

三地的共同點是：文憑菁英治國，
卻逃避結構改革。日本不敢改革勞動文化；
韓國不敢觸動房地產；台灣不敢面對低薪問題。
於是他們選擇了最簡單的辦法：撒錢補助。結果，
人民的生活沒有改善，出生率持續崩壞。

The three countries share one pattern: credentialed governance avoids structural reform.
Japan refuses to change work culture.
Korea refuses to touch real estate.
Taiwan refuses to confront low wages.
Thus, they choose the easiest path: cash subsidies.
The result? Citizens' lives remain unchanged, and fertility collapse accelerates.

啟示 Conclusion

東亞的少子化死局，揭示了文憑菁英治國的極限:
他們擅長設計補助方案，卻無法觸動體制。
人口結構的崩潰，不僅是社會危機，
更是對「分數治國邏輯」的徹底否定。

East Asia's demographic dead end exposes the limits of credentialed governance: elites excel at designing subsidies but cannot touch entrenched systems. Demographic collapse is not only a social crisis—it is a final verdict against score-driven governance.

第八章
德國的務實智慧

Chapter 8:
Germany’s Pragmatic Wisdom

2015 年，歐洲難民潮湧入，德國社會陷入激烈爭論。
有人恐懼，有人抗議，媒體的聲音此起彼落。
當時的總理梅克爾，並沒有立刻給出華麗的口號，
而是簡單地說了一句：「我們能做到（Wir schaffen das）。」
她並不是在展示自信，而是在提醒國民：政府有責任去
承擔挑戰，逐步解決問題。
這句話後來成為她政治風格的縮影——
務實、耐心、責任。

In 2015, as waves of refugees poured into Europe, Germany was thrown into fierce debates. Fear spread, protests erupted, media clamored. Chancellor Angela Merkel did not deliver a grandiose slogan. Instead, she simply said: “Wir schaffen das” (We can manage this). It was not a show of bravado but a reminder: government must shoulder responsibility and solve problems step by step. This phrase became emblematic of her style—pragmatism, patience, and responsibility.

梅克爾的政治智慧不在於她的博士學位，
而在於她把「治理」
視為一種務實的生活藝術。她既不是修辭家，
也不是理論家，而是能在危機中冷靜傾聽、
整合意見、逐步行動的領導者。

Merkel’s political wisdom lay not in her doctorate, but in her treatment of governance as a pragmatic art of living. She was neither a rhetorician nor a theorist but a leader who, in crises, listened calmly, integrated perspectives, and acted step by step.

案例分析 Real Cases

案例一：歐元危機中的平衡

在歐債危機期間，南歐國家瀕臨破產，北歐國家不願埋單。梅克爾並沒有用修辭劃清界線，而是不斷協商，尋找各方都能接受的平衡方案，最終維持了歐盟的完整。

During the Eurozone crisis, southern states teetered on bankruptcy while northern states resisted bailouts. Merkel did not use rhetoric to draw lines but negotiated tirelessly for compromise, preserving the EU's integrity.

案例二：難民危機中的承擔

2015 年，德國接收超過百萬難民。這個決定引發巨大爭議，但梅克爾承擔責任，不以恐懼為藉口，也不以仇恨為工具。她的立場不是情緒化的表態，而是務實的選擇：既然問題存在，就必須正面應對。

In 2015, Germany admitted over a million refugees. The decision was divisive, but Merkel bore responsibility—neither excusing inaction with fear nor weaponizing hate. Her stance was not emotional posturing but pragmatic choice: if the problem exists, it must be addressed.

案例三：疫情中的科學理性

在新冠疫情初期，梅克爾以科學家的冷靜，親自解釋病毒傳播的模型，說明「必須採取封鎖與防護措施」。她不用威嚇，而是用理性贏得信任。

At the start of COVID-19, Merkel, trained as a scientist, calmly explained viral transmission models and the necessity of lockdowns. She did not resort to fearmongering but won trust through reason.

梅克爾的力量，不來自「文憑光環」，而是來自「務實治理」。相比牛劍、常春藤的修辭家，她展現了另一種領導模式：不追求標準答案，而是追求可行的答案。

Merkel's strength stemmed not from "diploma prestige" but from "pragmatic governance." Compared to Oxbridge or Ivy rhetoricians, she embodied another model of leadership: not the perfect answer, but the workable answer.

德國的務實智慧提醒我們：真正的領導不是展示才華，而是承擔責任。梅克爾證明了「生命藝術家」如何超越「文憑蠢貨」，把治理化為一種穩定、持續的生活實踐。

Germany's pragmatic wisdom reminds us: true leadership is not about showcasing brilliance but shouldering responsibility. Merkel proved how an "artist of life" can surpass "diploma fools," turning governance into a steady, enduring practice of life.

第九章
烏拉圭的樸實總統

Chapter 9:
Uruguay’s Humble President

2010 年，當穆希卡就任烏拉圭總統時，國際媒體震驚地發現：他拒絕住進總統官邸，而是繼續住在首都郊區一棟簡陋的農舍裡。他沒有豪華座車，只有一輛破舊的大眾甲殼蟲。當記者問他為什麼過這樣的生活時，他回答：「我已經擁有足夠了。」這種態度，讓他贏得了「世界上最窮的總統」的稱號，但同時，也贏得人民最深的尊敬。

When José Mujica took office as Uruguay's president in 2010, the world was stunned to learn that he refused to move into the presidential palace. Instead, he remained in a modest farmhouse on the outskirts of Montevideo. His only car was a battered Volkswagen Beetle. When asked by journalists why he lived this way, he replied: "I already have enough." This lifestyle earned him the nickname "the world's poorest president," but also the deepest respect of his people.

穆希卡的力量，不在於他的演說技巧或學術背景，
而在於他以 生活的真誠與樸實 贏得了政治的正當性。
他展現出：治理不是炫耀，而是同理與承擔。

Mujica's strength did not lie in oratory or academic credentials, but in his authentic and humble way of living, which gave him political legitimacy. He showed that governance is not about display, but about empathy and responsibility.

案例分析 Real Cases

案例一：捐出九成薪水

穆希卡上任後，將總統薪水的九成捐出，
用於貧困者與社會計畫。他說：「國家需要的不只是政策，
而是實際的資源分享。」
這讓人民感受到，總統與他們站在一起。

Mujica donated 90% of his presidential salary to the poor and social programs. “What the country needs is not just policies, but real sharing of resources,” he said. Citizens felt their president stood with them.

案例二：大麻合法化與進步改革

在他的推動下，烏拉圭成為全球第一個將大麻全面
合法化的國家。他的理由不是理論，而是務實：
與其讓黑市壟斷，不如由政府管理以減少犯罪。
這展現了他以生活經驗，而非學術論文，
來解決問題的風格。

Under his leadership, Uruguay became the first country to fully legalize marijuana. His reasoning was pragmatic, not theoretical: better for the government to regulate it than leave it to the black market. This showed his style of solving problems with lived experience rather than academic papers.

案例三：以身作則的簡樸治理

穆希卡反對官僚的奢華與虛偽，強調政府應該過與人民相同的生活。這種以身作則的態度，使他的政策更具說服力，也讓社會信任重新建立。

Mujica opposed bureaucratic extravagance and insisted that government should live as ordinary people do. This example gave his policies credibility and helped restore trust in society.

與牛劍、常春藤的「文憑蠢貨」相比，
穆希卡證明：政治合法性不來自文憑，
而來自生活的真實。當英美政客忙著秀履歷、
背誦數據時，烏拉圭總統用一輛舊金龜車，
提醒世界什麼叫做「真正的治理」。

Compared to Oxbridge or Ivy “diploma fools,” Mujica proved that political legitimacy does not come from credentials but from authentic living. While Western elites flaunted résumés and recited numbers, Uruguay’s president, with his old Beetle, reminded the world what true governance means.

啟示
Conclusion

穆希卡的故事說明：
治理是一種生活的藝術，
而不是一場履歷比賽。真正的領導者，
不需要高學歷的光環，而需要與人民
同苦同甘的勇氣與誠懇。

Mujica's story shows that governance
is an art of living,
not a résumé contest. True leaders do not need
elite diplomas but the courage and sincerity to
share life with their people.

第十章
芬蘭的教育革命

Chapter 10:
Finland’s Educational Revolution

一位芬蘭老師對學生說：「今天沒有考試，
我們要去森林裡上課。」學生們驚訝又開心。
他們學習如何辨認植物、觀察動物，
並把所見所感記錄下來。
這不是「額外活動」，而是正規課程的一部分。
對芬蘭而言，教育不是考高分的機器，
而是培養完整的人生能力。

A Finnish teacher told her students: “No test today—we’re going to the forest for class.” The children were surprised but delighted. They learned to identify plants, observe animals, and record their impressions. This was not an extracurricular trip but a core part of the curriculum. For Finland, education is not a machine for producing high scores but a way of cultivating life skills.

核心論點 Core Argument

芬蘭的教育革命，是對「分數邏輯」的徹底反叛。
政府在 1970 年代開始推動改革，逐步取消全國性的排名考試，
將教育的重點轉向 平等、合作、生活能力。
結果，芬蘭在 OECD 的 PISA 測驗中一度名列世界前茅，
卻沒有製造出「分數怪物」，而是培養出兼具
知識與生活能力的公民。

Finland’s educational revolution was a rebellion against “score logic.” Starting in the 1970s, the government phased out nationwide ranking exams and redirected education toward equity, cooperation, and life skills. As a result, Finland topped OECD’s PISA assessments for years—not by producing “score monsters” but by cultivating citizens with both knowledge and life competence.

案例一：廢除排名考試
Case 1: Abolition of Ranking Exams

芬蘭取消了小學與國中階段的全國性排名考試，取而代之的是老師的日常評估與學生的自我反思。這讓學習從「考高分」轉向「真正理解」。

Finland abolished national ranking exams in primary and lower secondary school, replacing them with teachers' continuous assessment and students' self-reflection. Learning shifted from "scoring high" to "understanding deeply."

案例二：教育平等與免費制度
Case 2: Educational Equality and Free Schooling

芬蘭的教育完全免費，從小學到大學，連午餐也由政府提供。重點不是菁英篩選，而是確保所有人都能接受完整教育。這與東亞的「菁英迷思」形成鮮明對比。

Education in Finland is entirely free—from primary school to university, including school meals. The goal is not elite selection but ensuring everyone receives full education. This stands in stark contrast to East Asia's "elite obsession."

案例三：教師的專業與尊嚴
Case 3: Teachers' Professionalism and Dignity

芬蘭的教師幾乎都擁有碩士學位，卻不被迫成為「考試機器的操作員」。他們被信任為專業者，可以自由設計課程。這使教育真正回到「人的培養」。

Nearly all Finnish teachers hold master's degrees, yet they are not forced to be "operators of exam machines." Trusted as professionals, they design curricula freely. Education thus returns to cultivating people, not scores.

東亞的教育體系，往往把分數當唯一標準，造就了「文憑蠢貨」。芬蘭卻告訴世界：真正的教育不是製造精英，而是培養公民。這種思維差異，正是治理文化的根源不同。

East Asian systems often treat scores as the sole standard, producing "diploma fools." Finland shows the world: true education is not about creating elites but cultivating citizens. This divergence in thinking is at the root of different governance cultures.

啟示
Conclusion

芬蘭的教育革命，證明了「生活的藝術」也能成為
教育的核心。當學生學會合作、思考、理解現實，
他們長大後自然
能成為懂得治理的人。這正是東亞最欠缺的資源。

Finland’s educational revolution proves that the “art of life” can be the core of education. When students learn to cooperate, think, and engage with reality, they grow into adults capable of governance. This is the resource East Asia most desperately lacks.

第十一章
新加坡的規劃型治理

Chapter 11:
Singapore’s Engineered Efficiency

1965 年，新加坡剛獨立時，是一個資源貧乏的小島，失業率高，族群矛盾尖銳，甚至缺乏乾淨水源。許多觀察者認為它註定會失敗。然而，李光耀卻以「規劃型治理」徹底改寫了命運：打擊貪污、嚴格規劃城市、吸引外資。短短數十年，新加坡從貧困小島變成全球最有效率的城市國家。

In 1965, when Singapore became independent, it was a resource-poor island plagued by high unemployment, sharp ethnic tensions, and even a shortage of clean water. Many observers predicted its failure. Yet Lee Kuan Yew rewrote its destiny with “engineered governance”: eradicating corruption, strictly planning urban growth, and attracting foreign investment. Within decades, Singapore transformed from a struggling island to one of the world’s most efficient city-states.

新加坡的成功，不是因為文憑菁英的修辭，而是因為務實的規劃與制度設計。李光耀展現出：治理不是演說藝術，而是制度工程。

Singapore’s success did not come from credentialed elites’ rhetoric but from pragmatic planning and institutional design. Lee Kuan Yew demonstrated that governance is not the art of speeches but the engineering of systems.

案例分析 Real Cases

案例一：嚴格的反貪制度
Case 1: Strict Anti-Corruption System

李光耀建立獨立的反貪機構，賦予極大權限，任何人涉貪都必須接受調查。這使得新加坡迅速擺脫東南亞常見的貪污文化，建立廉潔的政府。

Lee Kuan Yew created an independent anti-corruption agency with sweeping powers, ensuring that anyone implicated faced investigation. This helped Singapore break free from the endemic corruption typical of Southeast Asia and build a clean government.

案例二：城市規劃與公共住房
Case 2: Urban Planning and Public Housing

新加坡透過政府主導的都市規劃，發展了完善的公共住房體系（HDB)。如今超過八成新加坡人住在政府規劃的組屋中，住房不再是社會不安的來源，而是穩定的基礎。

Through state-led urban planning, Singapore developed a comprehensive public housing system (HDB). Today, over 80% of Singaporeans live in government-designed flats, turning housing from a source of unrest into a foundation of stability.

案例三：吸引外資與教育改革
Case 3: Foreign Investment and Education Reform

李光耀政府積極吸引外資，並同步改革教育體系，培養技術型人才以滿足工業化需求。這種「教育與經濟掛鉤」的策略，使新加坡快速融入全球經濟。

Lee's administration actively courted foreign investment while reforming education to produce skilled workers for industrialization. This strategy of "linking education with the economy" allowed Singapore to integrate swiftly into the global economy.

與英國的牛劍修辭政治、美國的常春藤幻象相比，新加坡的故事提醒我們：真正的治理不是誰辯論贏，而是誰能規劃、執行、落實。西方菁英常停留在話語；新加坡則把治理當工程，讓制度自動運作。

Compared with Britain's Oxbridge rhetoric and America's Ivy illusion, Singapore's story shows us: true governance is not about who wins the debate but who plans, executes, and delivers.
Western elites often remain in words.
Singapore treated governance as engineering, making systems work automatically.

啟示
Conclusion

新加坡的經驗證明：治理是一種制度工程，
而不是文憑炫耀。
當政治菁英迷戀分數與修辭時，
人民需要的其實是能設計與執行的「工程師型領導者」。

Singapore's experience proves that governance is institutional engineering, not diploma display. While political elites indulge in scores and rhetoric, what citizens truly need are “engineer-leaders” who can design and implement systems.

第十二章
非洲的重建藝術

Chapter 12:
Rwanda’s Rebuilding Art

1994 年，盧安達爆發震驚世界的種族屠殺，短短一百天，
超過八十萬人遇害。整個國家幾乎化為廢墟：基礎設施被
毀，經濟癱瘓，社會撕裂。外界普遍認為，這個小國將無法
恢復。 然而，保羅．卡加梅在接任領導後，以堅毅與遠見
帶領盧安達走上重建之路。他沒有名校光環，卻展現了治理
的藝術：穩定社會、重建秩序、推動發展。

In 1994, Rwanda was devastated by a genocide that shocked the world: in just 100 days, over 800,000 lives were lost. The nation lay in ruins—its infrastructure destroyed, economy collapsed, and society torn apart. Many believed Rwanda could never recover.
Yet under Paul Kagame's leadership, Rwanda charted a path of reconstruction. Lacking elite diplomas, he nonetheless displayed the art of governance: stabilizing society, restoring order, and driving development.

卡加梅的治理告訴世界：真正的領導不是考試分數，
而是從廢墟中重建秩序的能力。 當文憑菁英陷於話術與數據時，
他以行動與堅持證明，領導是一門「生命的藝術」。

Kagame's leadership demonstrates that true governance is not about exam scores but the ability to rebuild order from ruins. While credentialed elites get lost in rhetoric and data, he proved through action and perseverance that leadership is an "art of life."

案例分析 Real Cases

案例一：重建秩序與治安
Case 1: Restoring Order and Security

屠殺後，盧安達最迫切的挑戰是安全。卡加梅領導的盧安達愛國陣線（RPF）迅速穩定局勢，拆解民兵組織，並建立可靠的治安體系。這為後續發展鋪下基礎。

After the genocide, Rwanda's immediate challenge was security. Kagame's Rwandan Patriotic Front (RPF) quickly stabilized the situation, dismantled militias, and established a reliable security system. This laid the groundwork for further progress.

案例二：反貪與廉潔政治
Case 2: Anti-Corruption and Clean Governance

卡加梅將反貪列為國家核心政策。他嚴格打擊貪污，提升政府透明度，使盧安達在非洲國家中，成為最廉潔、最有效率的政體之一。

Kagame made anti-corruption a central policy. He cracked down on graft and increased transparency, turning Rwanda into one of Africa's cleanest and most efficient governments.

案例三：經濟與科技的崛起
Case 3: Rise of Economy and Technology

卡加梅積極推動「盧安達願景 2020」，大力發展科技與基礎設施。首都基加利成為非洲最乾淨、安全的城市之一，盧安達也被譽為「非洲的星星」。

: Kagame advanced “Vision 2020,” prioritizing technology and infrastructure. Kigali became one of Africa’s cleanest and safest cities, while Rwanda earned a reputation as the “star of Africa.”

與動輒秀文憑的西方菁英不同，卡加梅的力量來自
「親身行動」而非「光鮮履歷」。
他證明了：治理不是炫耀，而是承擔。
這也是文憑蠢貨最缺乏的特質。

Unlike Western elites who flaunt credentials, Kagame’s strength came from action, not résumés. He proved that governance is not about display but about responsibility—the very trait most lacking among diploma fools.

啟示
Conclusion

盧安達的重建經驗，展現了治理的本質：領導者不需要耀眼的學歷，而需要直面最艱難現實的勇氣與決心。這種「重建的藝術」，正是任何社會在危機中最需要的資源。

Rwanda’s reconstruction shows the essence of governance: leaders do not need dazzling diplomas, but the courage and resolve to face the harshest realities. This “art of rebuilding” is the resource every society needs most in times of crisis.

第十三章
傾聽的力量

Chapter 13:
The Power of Listening

在德國某次地方社區會議上，一名居民激動地抱怨交通問題。
官員們準備好的簡報，原本要展示「數據與解決方案」。
但市長卻先放下投影筆記，耐心聽完居民的憤怒與擔憂，
並一一回應。事後，居民雖然並不完全滿意，但他們說：
「至少有人真的聽見我們了。」這種被傾聽的感受，
本身就是治理的一部分。

At a German town hall meeting, a resident angrily complained about traffic problems. Officials had slides ready to present "data and solutions." Yet the mayor first set aside his notes and listened patiently to the resident's frustration, responding point by point. Later, residents admitted they were not fully satisfied but said: "At least someone really heard us." The feeling of being heard is itself part of governance.

真正的治理，不在於領導者的「說」，而在於他們的「聽」。
文憑蠢貨 習慣於灌輸標準答案，把人民當學生；
生命的藝術家 則懂得傾聽，把治理視為對話。

True governance lies not in what leaders say,
but in what they hear.
Diploma fools impose standard answers,
treating citizens like students.
Artists of life listen, treating governance as dialogue.

案例分析 Real Cases

案例一：南非的真相與和解委員會
Case 1: South Africa's Truth and Reconciliation Commission

在種族隔離結束後，曼德拉與圖圖大主教推動「真相與和解委員會」，讓加害者與受害者都有機會敘述經歷。這種制度性的傾聽，避免了社會進一步的報復循環。

After apartheid, Nelson Mandela and Archbishop Desmond Tutu established the Truth and Reconciliation Commission, giving both victims and perpetrators a chance to tell their stories. This institutionalized listening prevented cycles of revenge.

案例二：德國的社區治理
Case 2: Germany's Local Governance

德國許多地方政府設有「居民諮詢會」，政策制定前必須先徵詢居民意見。雖然耗時，但這種傾聽過程提高了決策的合法性。

English: Many German municipalities have "citizens' advisory councils," requiring consultation before policy decisions. Though time-consuming, this listening process increases legitimacy.

案例三：台灣的太陽花運動後遺症
Case 3: Taiwan's Sunflower Movement Aftermath

2014 年太陽花運動後，年輕人對政府的不信任加深。
政客沒有真正傾聽，只是用更多「政策宣導」來應付，
結果社會裂痕依舊存在。
這顯示缺乏傾聽如何削弱民主。

After Taiwan's 2014 Sunflower Movement, distrust of government among youth deepened. Politicians failed to listen, responding instead with more "policy promotions." The social rift persisted, showing how lack of listening weakens democracy.

傾聽不是軟弱，而是治理的根基。
文憑蠢貨把治理當「單向灌輸」，因此失敗；
生命藝術家把治理當「雙向交流」，因此能建立信任。

Listening is not weakness but the foundation of governance. Diploma fools treat governance as "one-way imposition," and fail. Artists of life treat governance as "two-way dialogue," and build trust.

啟示Conclusion

治理的第一步，不是拿出解答，而是願意傾聽。
被傾聽的人，才會願意成為社會的一部分。真正的領導力，
從耳朵開始，而不是從文憑開始。

The first step of governance is not offering answers but listening. People who feel heard are more willing to participate in society. True leadership begins with ears, not diplomas.

第十四章
整合的能力

Chapter 14:
The Ability to Integrate

一位樂團指揮站在舞台上，面前是來自不同聲部的演奏者。
小提琴、中提琴、大提琴、銅管、木管，每一個聲音都獨立而尖銳。若各吹各調，必然混亂無比。但在指揮的整合下，這些聲音卻能合奏成一首完整的交響曲。
治理，就像指揮樂團一樣，不在於領導者自己會演奏，而在於能否整合眾聲。

A conductor stands on stage before musicians of different sections—violins, violas, cellos, brass, woodwinds. Each voice is distinct and sharp. Left uncoordinated, the result would be chaos. But under the conductor's guidance, these voices merge into a symphony. Governance is like conducting: it is not about the leader playing every instrument, but about integrating diverse voices.

整合是治理的核心能力。
文憑蠢貨 習慣以單一標準答案處理複雜問題；
生命藝術家 則懂得把不同利益與文化整合在一個框架裡。

Integration is the core capacity of governance.
Diploma fools rely on single "correct answers" to tackle complex issues.
Artists of life integrate diverse interests and cultures into a workable whole.

案例分析 Real Cases

案例一：歐盟的持續整合
Case 1: The Ongoing Integration of the European Union

歐盟由二十多個國家組成，各有語言、文化與利益衝突。若用「單一解答」處理，必然失敗。但透過協商與整合，歐盟雖然步履蹣跚，卻仍維持了和平與合作。
The European Union consists of over twenty nations, each with its own language, culture, and interests. A single answer would doom it. Yet through negotiation and integration, the EU—though stumbling—has preserved peace and cooperation.

案例二：馬來西亞的族群治理

Case 2: Ethnic Governance in Malaysia

馬來西亞由馬來人、華人與印度人構成。歷屆政府透過「社會契約」與多族群協商，避免了大規模衝突。雖然不完美，但這種整合能力，使多元社會得以勉強維繫。

Malaysia is composed of Malays, Chinese, and Indians. Through “social contracts” and interethnic negotiation, successive governments have avoided major conflict. Imperfect as it is, this integrative capacity has held a diverse society together.

案例三：南非的多元民主
Case 3: South Africa's Multiracial Democracy

曼德拉上台後，沒有選擇「黑人復仇」，而是推動多元民主。他整合不同族群的聲音，將國家帶出種族隔離的陰影。這種整合力，遠比任何演說更具力量。

When Nelson Mandela took power, he did not pursue "black revenge" but built a multiracial democracy. By integrating diverse voices, he led the nation out of apartheid's shadow. His ability to integrate was more powerful than any speech.

文憑蠢貨總以為政策是「解方公式」，
能代入數字得出唯一答案。
但現實世界是一場多聲部的交響曲，必須靠整合才能演奏。
缺乏整合力的領導者，只會把國家推入對立與僵局。

Diploma fools believe policies are "formula solutions," where numbers yield a single answer. But the real world is a polyphonic symphony that requires integration. Leaders without integrative ability drive nations into division and deadlock.

啟示
Conclusion

整合的能力，是治理的真正考驗。能傾聽是一回事，能把衝突與差異化為共識，才是更高一層的藝術。真正的領導者，是社會的指揮家，而不是解題的考生。

The ability to integrate is the true test of governance. Listening is one step; transforming conflicts and differences into consensus is a higher art. True leaders are conductors of society, not test-takers searching for the right answer.

第十五章
創造的勇氣

Chapter 15:
The Courage to Create

在二戰廢墟中，德國城市滿目瘡痍。人們不僅失去了房屋，
更失去了希望。
這時，市長們面對的不是「怎樣回到戰前」，
而是「如何創造一個全新的開始」。許多人選擇了重建與創造，
而不是逃避。這份勇氣，讓德國得以浴火重生。

After World War II, German cities lay in ruins. People had lost not only their homes but also hope. At that moment, mayors faced not the question of "how to return to the past," but "how to create a new beginning." Many chose rebuilding and creation over avoidance. That courage allowed Germany to rise from the ashes.

治理的最高境界，是創造。
文憑蠢貨 只會複製標準答案，停留在「避免錯誤」的層次；
生命藝術家 則敢於在混亂中開創新局，
把「不存在的答案」變成現實。

The highest level of governance is creation.
Diploma fools replicate standard answers, confined to "avoiding mistakes."
Artists of life dare to create in chaos, turning "nonexistent answers" into reality.

案例分析 Real Cases

案例一：以色列的創新國家
Case 1: Israel as a Startup Nation

在充滿戰爭威脅與資源匱乏的環境下，以色列選擇投入創新科技，培養出無數新創企業。這種「敢於創造」的精神，使它成為全球創新重鎮。

Amid constant threats of war and scarce resources, Israel invested in innovation and nurtured countless startups. This “courage to create” turned it into a global hub of innovation.

案例二：韓國的經濟奇蹟
Case 2: Korea’s Economic Miracle

1960 年代的韓國還是貧窮農業國，但領導者選擇了工業化與科技投資的道路，冒險推動出口導向政策。這種創造性的勇氣，使韓國成為世界第十大經濟體。

In the 1960s, Korea was still a poor agrarian society. Its leaders boldly pursued industrialization and export-led growth, taking risks in technology and manufacturing. This creative courage made Korea the world’s tenth-largest economy.

案例三：愛沙尼亞的數位國家
Case 3: Estonia's Digital Nation

蘇聯解體後的小國愛沙尼亞，選擇以「數位國家」作為重生策略。推動電子身分證、線上投票與數位政府服務，成為全球數位治理的先驅。

After the Soviet collapse, small Estonia chose to reinvent itself as a "digital nation." It introduced e-ID cards, online voting, and digital public services, becoming a global pioneer in e-governance.

分數治國，只能保證「不出錯」，卻無法引領社會走向未來。
唯有創造，才能讓一個國家在危機中重生。
文憑蠢貨缺乏勇氣，他們等待標準答案；
生命藝術家則憑著直覺與決心，勇於創造新答案。

Score-based governance ensures "no mistakes" but cannot lead societies into the future. Only creation allows nations to be reborn from crisis. Diploma fools lack courage, waiting for standard answers; artists of life rely on intuition and resolve, daring to create new ones.

啟示
Conclusion

創造的勇氣，是治理藝術的最高表現。
歷史一次又一次
告訴我們：國家並非靠文憑菁英的分數邏輯走出困境，
而是靠敢於創造的領導者，為人民開闢新路。

The courage to create is the highest expression of the art of governance. History shows again and again: nations do not escape crises through diploma elites' score logic, but through leaders bold enough to create new paths for their people.

結語
真正的領導是生活的藝術

Conclusion:
True Leadership Is the Art of Living

回顧本書，我們看到兩條迥異的道路。

一條，是「文憑蠢貨」的道路。他們依賴分數與文憑，把治理當成考卷，用修辭掩蓋無能，用補助替代改革。他們治下的國家，看似理性嚴謹，卻陷入人口崩潰、政策失靈、社會分裂。這條道路，製造的不是解決方案，而是幻象與失望。

另一條，是「生命藝術家」的道路。他們可能沒有耀眼的學歷，但懂得傾聽、整合與創造。他們把治理視為生活的延伸，而不是競賽的結果。德國的務實智慧、烏拉圭的樸實總統、芬蘭的教育革命、新加坡的規劃效率、盧安達的重建藝術，都告訴我們：真正的領導，是把抽象的國家責任，落實為人民可感的日常。
因此，真正的領導，不是考試的分數，
而是面對現實的勇氣；不是履歷的光環，
而是承擔的行動。
領導是一門生活的藝術。這門藝術，需要同理心、耐心與創造力，而非一紙文憑。

未來的世界，不需要更多「高分低能」的統治者，而需要更多懂得人性的藝術家。當我們看清這一點，我們也就能開始擺脫分數幻覺，迎向更具希望的治理之路。

Looking back through this book, we see two divergent paths.

One is the path of the diploma fools. They rely on scores and credentials, treating governance as an exam. They mask incompetence with rhetoric, substitute subsidies for reform. Under their rule, nations appear rational and rigorous but sink into demographic collapse, policy failure, and social fracture. This path produces not solutions but illusions and disappointment.

The other is the path of the artists of life. They may lack dazzling diplomas, yet they know how to listen, integrate, and create. They see governance as an extension of life, not the outcome of a competition. Germany's pragmatic wisdom, Uruguay's humble president, Finland's educational revolution, Singapore's engineered efficiency, Rwanda's rebuilding art—all show us that true leadership turns abstract national responsibility into concrete daily realities for people.

Thus, true leadership is not about exam scores but the courage to face reality; not about résumé prestige but the actions of responsibility. Leadership is an art of living. This art requires empathy, patience, and creativity—not a piece of paper.

The future does not need more "high-score, low-capacity" rulers. It needs more artists of life who understand humanity. Once we see this truth, we can begin to free ourselves from the illusion of scores and move toward a more hopeful path of governance.

作者簡介
About the Author

徐萍（Ping Xu），作家、鋼琴家、口譯員與政策改革倡議者，長年關注教育、長照、住房與稅制等制度性議題，並以「文憑蠢貨」與「生命藝術家」的對比觀點，批判當代菁英政治的盲點。她出版多部著作，涵蓋雙語童書與政策評論，結合個人生命經驗與國際視野，展現跨文化的深刻洞察。
2020 年疫情期間，她身處德國，親眼目睹一個國家如何以務實、耐心與制度信任來應對危機。這段經歷，讓她深刻體會：治理不是文憑的炫耀，而是生活的藝術。這份體悟，成為本書思想的核心基石。

Ping Xu is an author, pianist, interpreter, and policy reform advocate with a long-standing focus on systemic issues such as education, long-term care, housing, and taxation. She contrasts “diploma fools” with “artists of life” to critique the blind spots of elite-driven politics. Her published works span bilingual children’s literature and policy commentaries, weaving together personal experiences and global perspectives to offer cross-cultural insights.
During the pandemic in 2020, she lived in Germany and witnessed how a nation confronted crisis with pragmatism, patience, and institutional trust. That experience left a profound impression: governance is not about flaunting diplomas but practicing the art of life. This conviction became the intellectual foundation of this book.

《生活藝術家治國論》

The Art of Governance:

Why We Need Life Artists, Not Diploma Fools

前言
Preface

我們正處在一個治理失能的時代。文憑與分數被奉為最高價值，社會卻日漸陷入焦慮、冷漠與麻痺。

We are living in an era of failed governance. Diplomas and scores are worshiped as supreme values, yet society sinks deeper into anxiety, indifference, and paralysis.

分數怪物在教室裡誕生，文憑蠢貨在職場與政壇上得勢，技術官僚則佔據了國家核心。

Score monsters are born in classrooms, diploma fools rise in workplaces and politics, and technocrats occupy the very core of the state.

他們擁有數據，卻沒有靈魂；熟悉程序，卻無法共鳴；能夠複製，卻缺乏創造。

They command data but lack soul; they master procedures but cannot resonate; they replicate but cannot create.

結果是，制度逐漸僵化，人民逐漸沉默，社會逐漸失去希望。
As a result, institutions grow rigid, citizens fall silent, and societies lose hope.

這本書提出另一種可能：我們需要「生活藝術家」來治理國家。
This book proposes another possibility: we need “life artists” to govern our nations.

生活藝術家不是浪漫的空想家，而是能夠把生活經驗轉化為制度智慧的人。他們懂得觀察、具備想像、善於敘事、勇於創造。

Life artists are not romantic dreamers but people who transform lived experience into institutional wisdom. They observe keenly, imagine boldly, tell stories powerfully, and create courageously.

治理不是一份考卷，而是一門藝術。
Governance is not an exam—it is an art.

藝術家之所以重要，不是因為他們多情感，而是因為他們能看見別人看不見的細節，能想像別人不敢想像的未來，能將冷冰冰的制度轉化為有溫度的生活藍圖。

Artists matter not because they are more emotional, but because they see details others overlook, imagine futures others dare not, and transform cold institutions into living blueprints.

這本書將帶領讀者走過十二個章節，從分數怪物、文憑蠢貨，到技術官僚的冷血統治，再到生活藝術家的觀察力、想像力、敘事力與創造力，最後走向制度的重生。

This book will take readers through twelve chapters—from score monsters and diploma fools, to the cold-blooded rule of technocrats, to the observational, imaginative, narrative, and creative powers of life artists, and finally toward the rebirth of institutions.

它既是對當前制度的批判，也是對未來治理的邀請。

It is both a critique of current systems and an invitation to future governance.

願我們不再被文憑蠢貨所統治，
而能由生活藝術家打開新的時代。

May we no longer be ruled by diploma fools, but led into a new era opened by life artists.

第一章
分數怪物的養成

Chapter 1
The Making of Score Monsters

分數怪物
Score Monsters

當代教育制度下，孩子們從小就被迫進入競爭。
他們每天面對的不是知識的探索，而是分數的壓力。
In today's education system, children are forced into competition from an early age. What they face daily is not the joy of learning, but the pressure of scores.

他們被訓練去記憶、去背誦、去計算，目標只有一個：
考高分。分數成為評價一切的標準。
They are trained to memorize, recite, and calculate, with only one goal: to score high. Scores become the standard by which everything is judged.

於是，一批「分數怪物」誕生了。他們或許在考場上表現優異，卻在真實生活中失去敏感度與好奇心。
Thus, a generation of "score monsters" is born. They may excel in exams, yet in real life they lose sensitivity and curiosity.

分數怪物的特徵很明顯：
他們知道答案，但不知道問題的意義。
他們會算題目，但不會解決生活的矛盾。
他們能背定義，但無法創造新的觀點。
The traits of score monsters are clear:
They know the answers but not the meaning
of the questions.
They can solve exam problems
but not life's dilemmas.
They can recite definitions
but cannot create new perspectives.

教育體制告訴他們：只要分數高，就有未來。於是，
他們把學習當成工具，而不是習慣。
他們不再享受知識的美，
而是被迫成為分數的奴隸。

The system tells them: as long as you score high, you have a future. Thus, they treat learning as a tool, not a habit. They no longer enjoy the beauty of knowledge but are forced into slavery to scores.

當「分數怪物」進入社會，他們或許能憑藉文憑獲得位置，
卻缺乏面對現實的能力。他們看似聰明，
卻無法帶來真正的智慧。
When "score monsters" enter society, they may gain positions through diplomas but lack the ability to face reality. They appear intelligent, yet cannot bring forth true wisdom.

文憑蠢貨
Diploma Fools

當「分數怪物」長大進入社會，他們憑藉文憑的光環進入權力核心。於是，我們看到另一種現象：「文憑蠢貨」。
When “score monsters” grow up and enter society, they use the aura of diplomas to reach the centers of power. Thus, we see another phenomenon: the “diploma fool.”

文憑蠢貨憑藉名校的標籤取得權威，卻把治理當成考試，把政策當成標準答案。
Diploma fools gain authority through elite school labels, yet treat governance as an exam and policies as standard answers.

他們熟悉數據，會背理論，甚至能快速調出報告，但卻無法傾聽真實的聲音，無法整合不同的需求，更無法創造新的制度。
They are fluent in data, versed in theories, and quick with reports, but they cannot listen to real voices, cannot integrate diverse needs, and cannot create new institutions.

結果不是解決問題，而是讓問題更加僵化。
社會的矛盾在他們手中，往往只會被公式化、流程化，而不是被真正化解。
The result is not problem-solving but problem-freezing. Social contradictions, in their hands, are reduced to formulas and procedures rather than truly resolved.

文憑蠢貨最大的問題，在於缺乏靈魂。他們把治理
看成一份考卷，卻忘了人民不是考題，而是有血有淚的生命。

The greatest flaw of diploma fools is their lack of soul. They see governance as an exam paper, forgetting that people are not questions but lives of flesh and blood.

於是，國家被交給一群只會考試、不懂生活的人。
他們或許能維持表面的穩定，卻無法帶領社會走向未來。

Thus, the nation is entrusted to those who can pass exams but do not understand life. They may maintain surface stability but cannot lead society into the future.

從分數到文憑的惡性循環
From Scores to Diplomas: A Vicious Cycle

分數怪物與文憑蠢貨並不是孤立的兩群人，
而是同一條流水線上的不同階段。
Score monsters and diploma fools are not separate groups of people but different stages on the same assembly line.

孩子被迫成為分數怪物，為了考高分、進名校；
當他們長大後，就披上文憑的外衣，變成了文憑蠢貨。
Children are forced into becoming score monsters in order to score high and enter elite schools; once grown, they put on the robe of diplomas and transform into diploma fools.

這是一個惡性循環：分數製造文憑，文憑製造權威，
權威又鞏固了分數至上的制度。
This is a vicious cycle: scores produce diplomas, diplomas produce authority, and authority reinforces a system obsessed with scores.

教育因此失去了真正的目的，不再是培養獨立思考與創造力，
而是成為一條訓練順從與服從的流水線。
Thus, education loses its true purpose. It no longer cultivates independent thinking or creativity, but becomes a conveyor belt training obedience and conformity.

這樣的制度，不僅扼殺了個人潛力，
也讓整個國家陷入停滯。因為領導者來自文憑蠢貨，
他們無法引導社會應對新的挑戰。

Such a system not only stifles individual potential but also traps the entire nation in stagnation. Since its leaders are diploma fools, they cannot guide society to face new challenges.

最終，分數怪物與文憑蠢貨相互滋養，
讓教育變成一場空洞的競賽，
讓治理變成一場無靈魂的模仿。

In the end, score monsters and diploma fools feed each other, turning education into a hollow contest and governance into a soulless imitation.

第二章
技術官僚的誕生

Chapter 2
The Birth of Technocrats

技術官僚並不是憑空出現的，他們正是分數怪物與文憑蠢貨進入社會後的進化版本。
Technocrats do not emerge out of nowhere; they are the evolved form of score monsters and diploma fools after entering society.

當一個人習慣於在數據和標準答案中生存，他進入政府或企業後，也會用同樣的方式處理現實問題。
When a person is accustomed to surviving on data and standard answers, they carry the same approach into government or corporate life.

技術官僚的特徵，是用知識和程序去包裹一切。他們相信，只要流程設計完整，問題就能自動被解決。
The hallmark of technocrats is their tendency to wrap everything in knowledge and procedures. They believe that as long as the process is complete, problems will solve themselves.

然而，真實的社會從來不是教科書。它充滿了矛盾、情感、文化與歷史的糾結，遠遠超出公式可以涵蓋的範圍。
Yet real society is never like a textbook. It is full of contradictions, emotions, culture, and historical entanglements—far beyond the reach of formulas.

技術官僚之所以誕生，是因為教育制度與社會制度共同推動：教育培養了只懂分數與文憑的人，社會又獎賞這樣的人，把他們推向權力的位置。

The rise of technocrats is driven by both the education system and the social system: education produces people who know only scores and diplomas, while society rewards them by elevating them into positions of power.

於是，治理逐漸變成一種技術性的官僚化操作，
而不是一門有靈魂的公共藝術。
Thus, governance gradually transforms into a technocratic operation, stripped of soul, rather than a public art.

冷冰冰的專業化
The Cold Face of Professionalism

所謂「專業化」，在當代社會常常被奉為最高價值。
似乎只要冠上「專業」二字，就能自動取得正當性。

“Professionalism” is often upheld as the highest value in contemporary society. It seems that attaching the word “professional” to something automatically grants it legitimacy.

技術官僚正是這種價值觀的產物。他們把治理問題
拆解成一個個專業領域：教育交給教育專家，
醫療交給醫療專家，財政交給財經專家。

Technocrats are products of this value system. They divide governance into separate professional domains: education for education experts, healthcare for medical experts, finance for economic experts.

看似嚴謹，實則冰冷。因為社會問題往往跨越領域，
教育牽動家庭，醫療牽動財政，住房影響人口。
專業化的切割，反而讓整體失去了靈魂。

It looks rigorous but is in fact cold. Social problems often cut across domains: education affects families, healthcare affects finance, housing affects demographics. The compartmentalization of professionalism strips the whole of its soul.

專業化還有另一個後果：人民被排除在外。
政策被包裝成艱澀的專業語言，
讓普通人覺得自己沒有資格參與討論。

Professionalism has another consequence: it excludes the people. Policies are wrapped in esoteric language, making ordinary citizens feel unqualified to take part in the conversation.

於是，治理逐漸變成專家的遊戲，而不再是公共的事務。
這種冷冰冰的專業化，讓制度看似完美，
卻失去了與人民的共鳴。

Thus, governance gradually becomes a game for experts rather than a public matter. This cold professionalism makes institutions appear flawless, yet devoid of resonance with the people.

真正的治理，不能只有專業的冷冰冰數據，
還必須有藝術家的敏感與溫度。

True governance cannot rely solely on the cold data of professionals—it must also carry the sensitivity and warmth of artists.

制度設計的失衡
The Imbalance of Institutional Design

技術官僚最大的問題，不是他們缺乏知識，而是他們過度依賴知識，卻缺乏整體性的判斷。

The greatest problem of technocrats is not their lack of knowledge, but their overreliance on it, combined with a lack of holistic judgment.

他們設計制度時，習慣從單一角度出發：
財政部關注平衡預算，教育部關注升學率，
勞動部關注就業數字。每個領域各自為政，
導致整體制度失去平衡。

When designing institutions, they start from a single perspective: the Ministry of Finance focuses on balanced budgets, the Ministry of Education on admission rates, the Ministry of Labor on employment figures. Each field acts in isolation, leaving the overall system unbalanced.

這種「碎片化設計」，就像一座城市
只有交通部門規劃道路，卻沒有考慮住宅與綠地；
或醫院只追求病床數量，卻忽略病人的身心需求。

This "fragmented design" is like a city where the transportation department designs roads without considering housing and green spaces, or a hospital that pursues bed counts while ignoring patients' mental and physical needs.

失衡的制度帶來兩種後果：一方面，政策之間相互衝突；另一方面，人民感受不到制度的完整支持。

Unbalanced institutions produce two outcomes: on the one hand, policies clash with one another; on the other, people feel no comprehensive support from the system.

這也是為什麼許多國家在關鍵時刻顯得無能：因為制度像拼裝品，沒有靈魂也沒有整合。

This is why many nations appear powerless at critical moments: their institutions resemble assembled parts—soulless and unintegrated.

真正的制度設計，需要跨領域的眼光，需要能把教育、住房、醫療、財政串連起來的能力。這正是生活藝術家所具備的，而技術官僚所缺乏的。

True institutional design requires a cross-disciplinary vision—the ability to connect education, housing, healthcare, and finance. This is what life artists possess, and what technocrats lack.

第三章
從技術官僚到冷血統治

Chapter 3
From Technocrats to Cold-Blooded Rule

第一節：腦袋營運方式——堆棧 vs 工廠
Section 1: Two Modes of Mental Operation — Stack vs Factory

人的思考方式，粗略來看，可以分成兩種：
「堆棧」與「工廠」。
Human thinking, broadly speaking, can be divided into two modes: stack and factory.

堆棧腦袋的特徵，是不斷把知識、數據、理論一層層往上疊。這種腦袋就像一個倉庫，什麼都有存放，但缺乏加工。它擅長回憶與背誦，非常適合應付考試，卻難以應對新的挑戰。

The stack mind piles knowledge, data, and theories layer by layer. It is like a warehouse—everything is stored, but nothing is processed. It excels at recall and repetition, perfect for exams, yet struggles when facing new challenges.

當社會出現新的矛盾，堆棧腦袋習慣翻找「資料庫」尋找標準答案，若找不到就陷入焦慮與僵局。這正是技術官僚的典型思維：冷冰冰地調用數據，卻沒有創造力去開出新路。

When new contradictions arise, the stack mind searches its “database” for standard answers; when none exist, it falls into anxiety and paralysis. This is the hallmark of technocratic thinking: coldly calling up data, but lacking creativity to forge new paths.

工廠腦袋則截然不同。它像一座加工廠，能將經驗、觀察與感受，轉化為新的產出。它不只是存放知識，而是轉化知識。這意味著會犯錯，但每次失敗都能成為改善的契機。

The factory mind is entirely different. Like a workshop, it takes in experiences, observations, and emotions, and transforms them into new outputs. It does not merely store knowledge—it transforms it. Mistakes occur, but each failure becomes an opportunity for refinement.

這正是生活藝術家的思維。他們能把居民的痛苦轉化為制度設計，把日常的觀察變成治理的靈感。他們的大腦不是僵化的倉庫，而是有機的工廠。

This is the mindset of life artists. They transform community suffering into institutional design, turn daily observations into governance insights. Their minds are not rigid warehouses but organic factories.

第二節：技術官僚的冷血統治
Section 2: The Cold-Blooded Rule of Technocrats

技術官僚的腦袋，大多是「堆棧模式」。他們能快速調用數據、引用法條、背誦專家報告，看似專業嚴謹，實際上卻缺乏對人性的感受力。於是，我們逐漸看到一種冷血的治理模式。

The minds of technocrats are mostly "stack mode." They can quickly retrieve data, cite laws, and recite expert reports, appearing professional and rigorous, yet lacking sensitivity to human realities. What emerges is a governance style that is increasingly cold-blooded.

數據至上，忽略人心

技術官僚習慣用數字衡量一切：GDP 成長率、出生率、死亡率、醫療床位數。他們以為只要數據漂亮，政策就算成功。問題是，數字無法反映人心的破碎。

Data Above All, Humanity Forgotten

Technocrats measure everything in numbers: GDP growth rates, birth rates, death rates, hospital beds per capita. They assume that as long as the figures look good, policies succeed. The problem is that numbers cannot reflect broken human lives.

當照顧者因壓力過大而自殺，統計表上只是「一個死亡數」；
當年輕人因房價絕望放棄生育，
人口報表只是「一個下降率」；當病人因醫療失誤死亡，
制度文件只是「一個醫療糾紛案件」。

When a caregiver commits suicide under unbearable stress, the statistics record it as "one death." When young people abandon childbearing out of despair over housing, the demographic report shows only "a declining rate." When a patient dies from medical error, the system notes it coldly as "a malpractice case."

技術官僚的數據框架，把真實的痛苦稀釋
成抽象的百分比，
讓治理失去了溫度。

The technocrats' framework dilutes real suffering into abstract percentages, draining governance of warmth.

制度優先，生命次要

在技術官僚的思維裡，制度比人重要。他們相信規則與程序能解決一切。於是，當人被制度壓垮時，他們不是修正制度，而是要求人去適應制度。

Institutions First, Life Second

In technocratic thinking, systems outweigh people. They believe that rules and procedures can solve everything. Thus, when people are crushed by the system, they do not revise it—they demand people adapt.

長照政策不是幫助照顧者，而是訓練照顧者「更專業」；
教育政策不是釋放孩子的好奇心，而是增加更多「標準化測驗」；勞動政策不是讓家庭更自由，
而是把假期切割成冷冰冰的「幾日、幾小時」。
Long-term care policy does not support caregivers—it trains them to be "more professional." Education policy does not nurture curiosity—it adds more "standardized testing." Labor policy does not free families—it slices leave into sterile "days" and "hours."

這種治理，看似嚴密，實際上就是用制度去消耗人命。
This governance looks meticulous
but in reality consumes human lives.

治理的冷血本質

技術官僚不是壞人，他們只是「去人性化」的產物。
他們把人當成制度裡的零件，忘了每一個人都是有血有淚的生命。結果就是：政策愈來愈完美，人民卻愈來愈絕望。
The Essence of Cold-Blooded Rule
Technocrats are not villains; they are products of dehumanization. They treat people as interchangeable parts in a machine, forgetting that each individual is flesh and blood. The result: policies become ever more perfect, while people grow ever more desperate.

這就是冷血統治的本質——不是暴君的殘忍，
而是技術官僚的麻木。
This is the essence of cold-blooded rule—not the cruelty of tyrants, but the numbness of technocrats.

第三節：制度麻痺與社會的失語
Section 3: Institutional Paralysis and the Silence of Society

當文憑蠢貨與技術官僚主導治理，社會逐漸陷入一種危險狀態：制度麻痺。
When diploma fools and technocrats dominate governance, society gradually falls into a dangerous state: institutional paralysis.

制度麻痺的現象

所謂制度麻痺，就是大家都知道問題存在，但制度始終不動。即使有人呼籲改革，最終也被報告、程序與官僚流程拖延到失效。
The Phenomenon of Institutional Paralysis
Institutional paralysis means that everyone knows the problems exist, but the system remains unmoved. Even when calls for reform arise, they are delayed into irrelevance by endless reports, procedures, and bureaucratic processes.

房屋問題，大家罵了十年，價格仍然高漲；長照政策，喊了十年，照顧者依然孤立無援；少子化危機，討論了十年，出生率卻年年下降。
Housing has been criticized for a decade, yet prices keep soaring. Long-term care has been debated for a decade, yet caregivers remain unsupported. The fertility crisis has been discussed for a decade, yet birthrates keep falling year after year.

表面上會議一場接一場，文件一本接一本，但真實生活
沒有任何改善。這就是制度麻痺的典型景象。
On the surface, there are countless meetings and endless documents, but in real life, nothing changes. This is the classic picture of institutional paralysis.

社會的失語

當制度一再失靈，人民逐漸失去發聲的意願。因為他們發現，
呼喊沒有用、抗議沒有用、提案沒有用。
久而久之，社會進入一種「失語狀態」。

The Silence of Society

As institutions repeatedly fail, people gradually lose the will to speak out. They realize that shouting changes nothing, protesting changes nothing, proposing changes nothing. Over time, society slips into a state of silence.

年輕人選擇沉默，用「躺平」表達絕望；中年人選擇忍耐，
把痛苦轉化為冷漠；
老年人選擇放棄，不再期待體制能提供保障。
The young choose silence, expressing despair by “lying flat.” The middle-aged choose endurance, turning pain into indifference. The elderly choose resignation, no longer expecting protection from the system.

這種失語比抗爭更可怕，因為它意味著社會
已經放棄了對未來的想像。
This silence is more terrifying than protest, because it signals society’s abandonment of any vision for the future.

惡性循環

制度麻痺與社會失語互相強化：
政府因民眾沉默而更怠惰，
民眾因政府無能而更失望。最終，國家
進入低耗能的表面穩定，
實際上正在一點一滴瓦解。

A Vicious Cycle

Institutional paralysis and social silence reinforce each other: governments grow lazier as citizens fall quiet, and citizens grow more hopeless as governments prove ineffective. Eventually, the nation enters a low-energy state of surface stability, quietly disintegrating underneath.

這就是文憑蠢貨與技術官僚最致命的後果：
他們不僅無法解決問題，
還讓社會失去了語言與希望。

This is the most fatal consequence of diploma fools and technocrats: not only do they fail to solve problems, they also strip society of its voice and hope.

第四章
藝術家的觀察力

Chapter 4
The Observational Power of Artists

真正的治理，不是背誦理論，而是看見生活。
觀察力，正是生活藝術家最根本的能力。
True governance is not about reciting theories but about seeing life. Observation is the most fundamental ability of life artists.

文憑蠢貨也會「看」，但他們看到的是數據、報表與百分比。
他們的眼睛習慣於抽象，卻對生活的細節麻木。

Diploma fools also "look," but what they see are data, reports, and percentages. Their eyes are trained for abstractions yet numb to the details of life.

生活藝術家的「看」則不同。他們會注意到街角孤單的老人，
課堂上失去好奇心的孩子，過勞而沉默的工人。
這些細節，正是制度失靈的真實證據。

Life artists "see" differently. They notice the lonely elder on the street corner, the child who has lost curiosity in class, the worker silenced by overwork. These details are living evidence of institutional failure.

觀察不是終點，而是起點。生活藝術家懂得將
觀察轉化為制度靈感。

Observation is not the end but the beginning. Life artists know how to turn observation into institutional inspiration.

在日本的社區營造中，藝術家走訪家戶，傾聽需求，
才設計公共空間；在北歐教育改革中，
教師先觀察孩子如何遊戲，再設計課程；
在社會運動中，藝術家把痛苦轉化為
紀錄片與劇場，引發共鳴，推動改革。

In Japan's community building, artists visited households and listened before designing public spaces. In Nordic education reforms, teachers observed how children learned through play before writing curricula. In social movements, artists transformed suffering into documentaries and theater, evoking resonance and driving change.

國家不是考卷，而是一幅畫布。缺乏觀察力的治理者，
只會胡亂潑灑顏料，最後得到混亂與失真
唯有敏銳的觀察者，才能先看清紋理，再下筆描繪，
讓制度既有結構，也有溫度。

A nation is not an exam sheet but a canvas. Leaders without observational power splash paint blindly, producing only chaos and distortion. Only keen observers can see the texture before drawing the strokes, creating institutions with both structure and warmth.

第五章
創造力與想像力

Chapter 5
Creativity and Imagination

如果說觀察力讓生活藝術家看見真相，
那麼創造力與想像力，
則讓他們能夠打破僵局，開闢新路。

If observation allows life artists to see truth, then creativity and imagination enable them to break deadlocks and open new paths.

文憑蠢貨最擅長的就是模仿。他們模仿國外制度，卻忽視本土現實；模仿專家建議，卻缺乏整體視野；模仿數據模型，卻無法應對突發的危機。

Diploma fools excel at imitation. They copy foreign systems while ignoring local realities, follow expert recommendations without holistic vision, and replicate data models but fail to respond to sudden crises.

因此，他們的政策往往是拼裝品：
看似完整，實際上卻脆弱不堪。

As a result, their policies are often patchworks: seemingly complete, yet fragile at the core.

生活藝術家則完全不同。他們不滿足於複製，而是能將零散的元素編織成新的格局。他們有空間感，也有突破力。

Life artists, by contrast, are never content with copying. They weave scattered elements into new patterns, possessing both spatial sense and breakthrough power.

在教育上，他們不是追問如何提高分數，而是創造能讓孩子熱愛學習的環境；在住房上，他們不是計算補助額度，而是重新設計城市空間；在長照上，他們不是增加機構床位，而是想像跨世代共生的社區。

In education, they do not ask how to raise scores but how to create environments where children love learning. In housing, they do not calculate subsidies but redesign urban spaces. In long-term care, they do not add institutional beds but imagine intergenerational communities.

所有偉大的改革，都是從想像力開始的。
當人們說「不可能」或「太理想化」時，
往往正是新制度的萌芽時刻。

Every great reform begins with imagination. When people say “impossible” or “too idealistic,” it is often the very moment when a new system germinates.

全民基本收入曾被嘲笑為烏托邦，如今已在多國試驗；
公共醫療曾被視為荒唐，如今是現代社會的標配；
女性投票權曾被認為顛覆傳統，如今卻是常識。

Universal Basic Income was once mocked as utopian—today it is tested in multiple countries. Public healthcare was once seen as absurd—today it is a standard of modern societies. Women’s suffrage was once considered radical—today it is common sense.

沒有想像力，人類就困在舊制度裡；
唯有想像力，才能讓治理超越框架。
Without imagination, humanity remains trapped in old systems; only imagination allows governance to transcend boundaries.

生活藝術家的創造力，不是個人表演，而是集體參與。
他們懂得打開公共空間，邀請群眾共創。
治理，本質上就是一場社會的集體藝術。

The creativity of life artists is not personal performance but collective participation. They know how to open public spaces and invite co-creation. Governance, at its core, is a collective art of society.

第六章
共鳴與敘事

Chapter 6
Resonance and Storytelling

如果說觀察力讓生活藝術家看見真相，
想像力讓他們打破舊局，那麼共鳴與敘事
，就是他們帶領群眾同行的關鍵。

If observation allows life artists to see truth, and imagination enables them to break old structures, then resonance and storytelling are what allow them to lead people along the journey.

文憑蠢貨不是不會說話，他們的演講往往充滿數據
與專業術語，卻缺乏溫度。
他們的語言像教科書段落，冷冰冰，沒有情感。

Diploma fools are not silent; their speeches are often filled with data and jargon, but they lack warmth. Their language reads like textbook paragraphs—cold and emotionless.

因此，他們雖然在說，卻沒有人在聽。

Thus, they may be speaking, but no one is truly listening.

生活藝術家的敘事完全不同。他們懂得用故事與比喻，
讓人與人之間產生連結。

Life artists tell stories differently. They know how to use narratives and metaphors to create connections among people.

當他們談長照，不是從床位數開始，
而是講一位照顧者的孤單；
當他們談住房，不是只說供需曲線，
而是描繪一對年輕夫妻的掙扎；當他們談教育，
不是強調排名，而是分享孩子如何重新找回學習的熱情。

When they discuss long-term care, they do not begin with bed counts but with the loneliness of a caregiver. When they talk about housing, they do not cite supply-demand curves but describe a young couple's struggles. When they speak of education, they do not emphasize rankings but share how a child rediscovered joy in learning.

這些故事不是描述，而是召喚。
人們會感覺到：「這和我有關」。
These stories are not mere descriptions—they are invitations. People feel: "This concerns me."

群眾不是被數據說服，而是被情感觸動。
當故事能引發共鳴，人們才願意行動。
People are not persuaded by data but moved by emotion. When a story resonates, people are willing to act.

治理需要故事的靈魂。沒有敘事的國家，
就像一台無聲的機械。
Governance needs the soul of story. A nation without narratives is like a silent machine.

唯有生活藝術家，能把制度變成故事，
把政策變成群眾共同的人生篇章。
Only life artists can transform institutions into stories, and policies into chapters of collective human life.

第七章
教育：
培養終身學習者，
而非分數奴隸

Chapter 7
Education:
Cultivating Lifelong Learners,
Not Score Slaves

教育是所有制度的起點。然而，在今日社會，
教育早已被分數與排名綁架。

Education is the foundation of all institutions. Yet in today's society, education has long been hijacked by scores and rankings.

孩子從小被迫進入競爭，學習不再是探索，
而是考高分、進名校、拿文憑。

Children are forced into competition from a young age. Learning is no longer about exploration, but about scoring high, entering elite schools, and obtaining diplomas.

於是，我們看到孩子失去了好奇心，卻練就了應付考試的技巧；
家長焦慮於成績，忽略了陪伴與啟發；
學校追逐升學率，卻犧牲了孩子的天性。

Thus, children lose curiosity but master test-taking skills; parents obsess over grades and neglect companionship and inspiration; schools chase admission rates at the cost of children's nature.

這樣的教育，培養的不是學習者，而是「分數奴隸」。
Such education does not cultivate learners but "score slaves."

生活藝術家對教育的理解，與文憑蠢貨完全不同。對他們而言，
教育的目的不是考高分或拿文憑，而是培養終身學習者。

Life artists see education entirely differently. For them, the goal of education is not to score high or obtain diplomas, but to cultivate lifelong learners.

學習應該是一種生活習慣，而不是競賽；
真正的學習來自探索與實踐，而不是死記硬背。
Learning should be a way of life, not a competition. True learning comes from exploration and practice, not rote memorization.

芬蘭的教育改革就是例子：取消繁重的考試與排名，強調學習的樂趣與合作。孩子不是被分數驅動，而是被興趣吸引。
Finland's education reform is an example: abolishing heavy exams and rankings, emphasizing joy in learning and collaboration. Children are driven not by scores but by curiosity.

教育不是工廠流水線，而是藝術的創作過程。每個孩子都是獨特的素材，需要被用心雕琢，而不是一體裁切。
Education is not an assembly line but an artistic process. Each child is unique material, to be carefully shaped, not cut into uniform molds.

唯有這樣的教育，才能孕育出真正的生活藝術家，
而不是文憑蠢貨。
Only such education can nurture true life artists rather than diploma fools.

教育的最終目標，不是送孩子進名校，
而是讓每個人一生都能保持學習的熱情。
The ultimate goal of education is not to funnel children into elite schools but to ensure that everyone keeps a passion for learning throughout life.

當一個社會充滿終身學習者，它就能擁有面對未來的韌性。
When a society is full of lifelong learners, it gains the resilience to face the future.

第八章
住房：
讓家成為生活的藝術空間

Chapter 8
Housing:
Making Homes the Artistic Space of Life

在文憑蠢貨的治理邏輯裡，房子常被簡化為數字：
價格、利率、貸款額度、供需曲線。
In the logic of diploma fools, housing is reduced to numbers: prices, interest rates, mortgage amounts, supply-demand curves.

因此，住房政策變成一場冷冰冰的財務計算，
房子被視為投資標的，而不是承載生活的空間。
Thus, housing policy becomes a cold financial calculation, and houses are treated as investment vehicles rather than spaces that carry life.

結果是，高房價壓垮年輕人，空屋閒置無人敢住，
社會資源被鎖死在鋼筋水泥裡。
The result is skyrocketing prices crushing young people, vacant homes left unused, and vast social resources locked in concrete and steel.

生活藝術家對「家」的理解完全不同。家不是資本，
而是生活的舞台，是孩子成長的土壤，是照顧者的庇護，
是老人安度晚年的依靠。
Life artists understand "home" differently. A home is not capital but the stage of life, the soil where children grow, the shelter for caregivers, and the anchor for elders in their final years.

如果一個年輕家庭為了貸款無法生養，這不是真正的家；
如果一個照顧者沒有喘息空間，這個家就是牢籠；
如果老人孤單困在高樓裡，這不是安居，而是被遺棄。

If a young family cannot have children because of crushing mortgages, it is not truly a home. If a caregiver has no respite, the home becomes a prison. If an elder is left isolated in a high-rise, it is not secure living but abandonment.

生活藝術家的住房觀，會將政策從數字轉向人性：
社會住宅不是收容所，而是共享資源；城市不是投機市場，
而是社區與文化的延伸。

The life artist's view of housing shifts policy from numbers to humanity: social housing is not a shelter but a shared resource; cities are not speculative markets but extensions of community and culture.

在丹麥與荷蘭，社會住宅以高品質設計著稱，
讓人人住得有尊嚴；在新加坡，公共住宅融合社區設施，
促進世代交流。

In Denmark and the Netherlands, social housing is known for high-quality design, ensuring dignity for all; in Singapore, public housing integrates community facilities to foster intergenerational exchange.

在台灣，若能將退場學校用地改造為社會住宅，
就能把「教育的遺址」變成「生活的起點」。
In Taiwan, transforming decommissioned school lands into social housing could turn “abandoned sites of education” into “new beginnings of life.”

治理住房，最終不是計算多少房子，
而是創造什麼樣的生活空間。
Ultimately, housing governance is not about calculating how many houses but about creating what kind of living spaces.

文憑蠢貨看到的是市場與數據；
生活藝術家看到的則是生命與故事。
Diploma fools see markets and data; life artists see lives and stories.

唯有讓每個人都有一個能安身立命的家，國家才能健康發展。
家，不應只是交易，而應是一種生活藝術。
Only when everyone has a home to live in dignity can a nation truly thrive. A home should not be just a transaction but a work of life art.

第九章
長照與醫療：制度的溫度

Chapter 9
Long-Term Care and Healthcare: The Warmth of Institutions

在技術官僚的治理下，長照與醫療常常被公式化、數據化：床位數、照顧時數、住院天數、醫療點數。
Under technocratic governance, long-term care and healthcare are often reduced to formulas and data: number of beds, caregiving hours, hospital stays, medical points.

這些數字或許在報告中漂亮，卻忽略了最根本的意義：制度是為了守護人。
These numbers may look impressive in reports, but they ignore the fundamental purpose: institutions exist to protect people.

當照顧者因壓力崩潰，當病人因錯誤治療喪命，體系卻只是冷冰冰地紀錄「一個案件」。
When a caregiver collapses under stress, or a patient dies from medical error, the system records it coldly as “one case.”

文憑蠢貨以為解決長照問題的方法，是訓練照顧者更專業；卻忘了照顧者本身正在被制度消耗。
Diploma fools think the solution to the care crisis is to train caregivers to be more professional, forgetting that caregivers themselves are being consumed by the system.

一位女性同時照顧失能父母與年幼孩子，
她需要的是支持與喘息，而不是一本更厚的手冊。

A woman caring for both disabled parents and young children needs support and respite, not a thicker manual.

一名外籍移工日夜輪班照護老人，他需要的是法律保障，
而不是更多技能課程。

A migrant worker caring for elders around the clock needs legal protections, not more training modules.

照顧者不是機器，他們的身心會被耗盡。
當政策只要求他們「更專業」，制度就是在用生命換制度。

Caregivers are not machines; their bodies and minds can be exhausted. When policies only demand they become "more professional," the system is essentially trading lives for its own survival.

生活藝術家看到的不是指標，而是具體的人。
他們會設計喘息服務，推動社區共養，
把醫療當作陪伴與治療的結合。

Life artists do not see indicators but people. They design respite services, promote community-based care, and treat healthcare as a union of companionship and cure.

醫療不是單純的技術，而是信任的關係。當醫患互動被簡化為同意書、檢查單、保險給付，人就消失在流程裡。

Healthcare is not merely technology but a relationship of trust. When doctor-patient interaction is reduced to consent forms, test orders, and insurance reimbursements, people vanish into procedures.

生活藝術家的醫療觀，會把「病人」還原成「人」，讓治療過程成為合作，而不是命令。

The life artist’s view of healthcare restores the “person” in the “patient,” making treatment a collaboration rather than a command.

制度的溫度，就是人性的溫度。冷血的制度會讓社會絕望；有溫度的制度，才能讓人感受到被接住、被理解、被支持。

The warmth of institutions is the warmth of humanity. Cold systems breed despair; warm systems make people feel held, understood, and supported.

第十章
財政與稅制：制度設計的藝術

Chapter 10

Finance and Taxation: The Art of Institutional Design

在文憑蠢貨的眼中，財政與稅制只是數字遊戲：
預算是加減乘除，稅收是百分比調整，赤字只是報表上的紅字。
In the eyes of diploma fools, finance and taxation are nothing but number games: budgets are addition and subtraction, taxes are percentage shifts, deficits are red figures on spreadsheets.

因此，他們的改革往往流於表面：多收一點，少花一點，
卻從未觸及制度的本質。

Thus, their reforms remain superficial: raise a little here, cut a little there, never addressing the essence of institutions.

生活藝術家對財政的理解，卻完全不同。對他們而言，
財政不只是收支平衡，而是一種社會共創的設計。

Life artists view finance differently. For them, it is not mere balance of income and expenses, but a design of social co-creation.

稅收不是懲罰，而是集體投資；預算不是分餅，
而是共同生活的藍圖。

Taxes are not punishments but collective investments; budgets are not slices of pie but blueprints for shared life.

真正的財政設計，應該讓人民覺得公平，願意參與；好的稅制，
應該能自動調節社會資源，而不是年年補漏洞。

True financial design should feel fair, inviting participation. A good tax system should regulate resources automatically, not require annual patchwork.

生活藝術家的稅制思維，會減輕中產階級的稅負，
引入穩定透明的消費稅制，並抑制投機型資本收益。

The life artist's approach to taxation lightens the burden on the middle class, introduces stable and transparent consumption-based taxes, and restrains speculative capital gains.

財政制度的設計，本質上是一門藝術。就像建築師設計城市，
不是只計算磚瓦，而是考慮人如何生活。

The design of fiscal systems is, at its core, an art. Like an architect designing a city, it is not about counting bricks but about how people will live.

文憑蠢貨看財政，是冷冰冰的算式；生活藝術家看財政，
則是一首集體交響曲。

Diploma fools see finance as cold arithmetic; life artists see it as a collective symphony.

每一個稅種、每一筆支出，就像交響樂的聲部，
必須彼此協調，才能奏出和諧樂章。

Each tax and expenditure is like a section of the orchestra, needing harmony to produce music.

缺乏藝術感的制度設計，只會發出機械的雜音；帶有藝術性的制度設計，才能讓財政成為支撐社會的樂器，
而不是壓垮人民的枷鎖。

Systems without artistry generate mechanical noise; systems with artistry make finance an instrument that sustains society, not a shackle that crushes its people.

第十一章
人口結構崩潰與制度想像

Chapter 11
Demographic Collapse and Institutional Imagination

人口結構的崩潰，是比金融風暴更安靜卻更致命的危機。
出生率下滑、老齡化加速、勞動人口萎縮，
悄悄吞噬一個國家的未來。

Demographic collapse is a quieter yet deadlier crisis than financial crashes. Falling birthrates, rapid aging, and shrinking workforces silently consume a nation's future.

日本已經陷入高齡化的重壓；韓國與台灣成為
「人口塌陷區」；歐洲則同時面臨銀髮社會與移民整合的壓力。

Japan has been crushed under the weight of aging; South Korea and Taiwan have become "population collapse zones"; Europe faces the dual strain of silver societies and immigrant integration.

文憑蠢貨的對策，通常只是補助或獎勵：發現金鼓勵生育，
多建安養機構，或引進移工。

The typical response of diploma fools is subsidies or incentives: cash bonuses for births, more nursing homes, or importing migrant workers.

這些方法看似積極，實則頭痛醫頭，無法觸及制度根本。

These measures look proactive but are stopgaps, failing to address systemic roots.

生活藝術家則會提出全新想像：教育上，讓孩子、青年、
老人共享空間；住房上，將閒置空屋轉化為跨世代社區；
長照上，把照顧視為全社會共同責任；
財政上，設立人口調節基金，以創新稅制應對挑戰。
Life artists offer new visions: in education, sharing spaces among children, youth, and elders; in housing, converting vacant homes into intergenerational communities; in care, redefining caregiving as a collective duty; in finance, creating population adjustment funds supported by innovative taxation.

人口崩潰沒有現成答案，它不是教科書題目，
而是需要想像力的挑戰。
Demographic collapse has no ready-made answer. It is not a textbook question but a challenge requiring imagination.

歷史告訴我們，每一次制度轉型都與人口變動有關。
今日的危機，也可能是制度更新的契機。

History shows us that every institutional transformation is linked to demographic change. Today's crisis may likewise be an opportunity for renewal.

若只是補助拖延，國家只會衰亡；若敢於以藝術家的想像回應，
則有可能開啟文明的新篇章。
If we only delay with subsidies, nations will decline; if we dare to respond with the imagination of artists, we may open a new chapter of civilization.

人口結構的崩潰，不必然意味國家崩潰，它也可能是
重生的契機。關鍵在於我們是否擁有制度的想像力。
Demographic collapse does not necessarily mean national collapse; it may also be the chance for rebirth. The key lies in whether we possess the imagination for new institutions.

第十二章
治理作為生活藝術

Chapter 12
Governance as the Art of Life

在文憑蠢貨的眼中，治理是一份考卷：制定法條、編列預算、解讀數據、完成KPI。

In the eyes of diploma fools, governance is an exam: drafting laws, allocating budgets, interpreting data, achieving KPIs.

但真正的治理，必須是一門藝術。它需要觀察、想像、共鳴與創造；需要對人性有感，對制度有靈魂。

But true governance must be an art. It requires observation, imagination, resonance, and creativity; it requires sensitivity to humanity and a soul for institutions.

生活藝術家不是理想化的浪漫主義者，而是能將生活經驗轉化為制度智慧的人。

Life artists are not idealistic dreamers but those who transform lived experience into institutional wisdom.

他們懂得：教育要培養終身學習者，而非分數奴隸；
住房要讓人安身立命，而非投機炒作；
長照與醫療要有溫度，而非冷冰冰的流程；
財政要是共創，而非懲罰；人口危機要是契機，而非死局。

They understand: education must cultivate lifelong learners, not score slaves; housing must provide dignity, not speculation; care and healthcare must have warmth, not cold procedures; finance must be co-creation, not punishment; demographic crises must be opportunities, not dead ends.

治理不是權力的壟斷，而是生活的延伸。
它不應只是少數人的專利，而應是全體社會的共同創作。

Governance is not the monopoly of power but the extension of life. It should not be the privilege of a few but the collective creation of society.

文憑蠢貨留下的是僵化、冷血與失語；生活藝術家帶來的，則是創造、希望與共鳴。

Diploma fools leave behind rigidity, coldness, and silence; life artists bring forth creativity, hope, and resonance.

唯有當治理被理解為生活藝術，人類才能走出制度麻痺，邁向一個有溫度、有希望、有創造力的新時代。

Only when governance is understood as the art of life can humanity escape institutional paralysis and step into a new era of warmth, hope, and creativity.

作者簡介
About the Author

徐萍（Ping Xu），作家、鋼琴家、口譯員與政策改革倡議者，長年關注教育、長照、住房與稅制等制度性議題，並以「文憑蠢貨」與「生命藝術家」的對比觀點，批判當代菁英政治的盲點。她出版多部著作，涵蓋雙語童書與政策評論，結合個人生命經驗與國際視野，展現跨文化的深刻洞察。2020 年疫情期間，她身處德國，親眼目睹一個國家如何以務實、耐心與制度信任來應對危機。這段經歷，讓她深刻體會：治理不是文憑的炫耀，而是生活的藝術。這份體悟，成為本書思想的核心基石。

Ping Xu is an author, pianist, interpreter, and policy reform advocate with a long-standing focus on systemic issues such as education, long-term care, housing, and taxation. She contrasts “diploma fools” with “artists of life” to critique the blind spots of elite-driven politics. Her published works span bilingual children’s literature and policy commentaries, weaving together personal experiences and global perspectives to offer cross-cultural insights.
During the pandemic in 2020, she lived in Germany and witnessed how a nation confronted crisis with pragmatism, patience, and institutional trust. That experience left a profound impression: governance is not about flaunting diplomas but practicing the art of life. This conviction became the intellectual foundation of this book.

www.ingramcontent.com/pod-product-compliance
Lightning Source LLC
LaVergne TN
LVHW100324210926
848480LV00003B/1248
9798349558665